DÜNGEONMEISTER

A DRINK MASTER'S GUIDE

DÜNGEONMEISTER

A DRINK MASTER'S GUIDE

75 EPIC RPG COCKTAIL RECIPES TO SHAKE UP YOUR CAMPAIGN

 JEF ALDRICH & JON TAYLOR

Adams Media
New York   London   Toronto   Sydney   New Delhi

Adams Media
An Imprint of Simon & Schuster, Inc.
100 Technology Center Drive
Stoughton, MA 02072

First Adams Media hardcover edition December 2020

ADAMS MEDIA and colophon are trademarks of Simon & Schuster.

For information about special discounts for bulk purchases, please contact Simon & Schuster Special Sales at 1-866-506-1949 or business@simonandschuster.com.

The Simon & Schuster Speakers Bureau can bring authors to your live event. For more information or to book an event contact the Simon & Schuster Speakers Bureau at 1-866-248-3049 or visit our website at www.simonspeakers.com.

Interior design by Michelle Kelly
Interior images by Priscilla Yuen, Claudia Wolfe, and Frank Rivera

Manufactured in the United States of America

9   2022

Library of Congress Cataloging-in-Publication Data has been applied for.

ISBN 978-1-5072-1465-7
ISBN 978-1-5072-1466-4 (ebook)

Always follow safety and commonsense cooking protocols while using kitchen utensils, operating ovens and stoves, and handling uncooked food. If children are assisting in the preparation of any recipe, they should always be supervised by an adult.

Contents

Introduction

Welcome to *Düngeonmeister*, a book where fantasy role-playing meets cocktail craft. One of the greatest things about role-playing is the way that it brings people together. A group of adults with different schedules all making time to get together and gather around a table is a kind of magic in and of itself. So we thought, why not make those get-togethers a true event with themed drinks to entertain and amuse your fellow players? Whether you're new to role-playing games or a grognard who's played for years, you can find the right drink (or drinks) for you. You don't even need to be role-playing. You can be the big hero at any nerdy get-together for board game nights, movie night, or even a simple hangout.

In this book, you will find seventy-five drink recipes: an assortment of different flavors and types of drinks, shots, punches, and cocktails. There should be something for everyone at the table: from those who want their drinks sweet and fruity, to those who want a spicy or bitter sharpness, and even those who just want to be able to min-max their alcohol consumption. We've included a section that tells you what basic alcohols and bar tools you'll need to keep yourself and your fellow gamers in tip-top condition. We've also included humorous sidebars for all of our recipes to provide plenty of entertainment and mirth.

We've added a handy Complexity rating on the different recipes so you'll know how much effort goes into them. Not everyone is willing to break out the blender or lovingly craft their own honey syrup. The lower-Complexity recipes just require the ingredients you plan to mix together and maybe a shaker to mix them all up. For the adventurous sort who wants to dive right into the deep end, our high-Complexity drinks will have you brewing your own tea or special-ordering powders for those mesmerizing special effects.

The book's eight chapters range from characters to classes to skills—plenty of room for you to match your drink to the phase of the game you're in. For instance, if you're rolling up a dwarven bard, you might want to have a Dwarven Forge by your elbow. If you're struggling through a dank swamp, pursued by rotting zombies, sipping a Black Mana will probably make you feel better (although you still better outrun the zombies).

So come along! Don't stand at the back of the party. It's time to eat, drink, and roll d20s.

Tavern Basics

It's only natural that epic quests begin in taverns. There's a sense of camaraderie; warmth from the hearth; simple, well-cooked meals; and, of course, copious tankards of fortifying alcohol. It's a rookie mistake to take these simple pleasures for granted, and if you're feeling like taking your game up to the next level of realistic verisimilitude, then why not set up your own pregame tavern? With our help, you'll be slinging characterful cocktails and potent potions that help infuse a little more spirit (and a little more spirits) into your dungeon adventures.

In this section you'll find:

- The basic alcohols you need for the drinks in this book
- A list of mixers
- The essential bar tools to make drinks

With all this, you'll be ready to plunge right in (so to speak!) to the drinks in the rest of the book. But what should your tavern include (besides plenty of adventurers and mysterious old men muttering to themselves in a corner)?

Essential Spirits for Tavern Keeping

All effective bars begin with a collection of spirits that forms the basis of mixology. Perhaps while setting up a place for dwarves or half-orcs, one can get away with ales ranging from strong to unpleasant, but if plans stray toward entertaining other players at the tavern table, it's best to start with a collection of the classics. Otherwise you'll find yourself in the unenviable position of trying to sling glasses of orange juice and sweet and sour mix to less than appreciative patrons and friends.

Vodka

Vodka is invariably the most used spirit in the bar. It's the go-to for cocktail making, and you'll find it in a majority of cocktail recipes. Distilled most commonly from grain or potato starch (but in reality can be made from nearly anything floral), vodka's claim to fame is a lack of flavor, meaning it can add a kick without adding a note.

Gin

Gin, similar to vodka, is a distilled spirit, though instead of lacking flavor, it has a lot of potential flavors. Gin is an exceptionally broad category of like spirits, which all feature juniper berry as a flavor note in common (and often not much else). You'll note throughout this guide that above any other basic spirit, gin is accompanied by the most type restrictions. In most recipes that call for gin, you can use any type you want—the exception being sloe gin. Blue or sapphire gin is a color choice. Sloe gin, however, is flavored by a sour little blue fruit known as a blackthorn, which changes its flavor profile from other gin immensely, and also makes it the alcohol with the best flavor profile to steal for character names. Unless otherwise noted, recipes that call for gin can use any gin you have on hand. If the recipe calls for something more specific, we'll be sure to say so.

Rum

Through the power of sugarcane (molasses or syrup), rum picks up deep, toasty sugar flavors. Beyond this, it can be difficult to ascribe any major catchall descriptions to rum, in no small part because few countries can agree on what rum even is! For our purposes, rum is generally either silver (clear) or spiced (some variation of a darker gold or caramel). It is also the perfect libation to add authenticity to adventures set on the high seas. Just keep it away from the powder barrels, please.

Tequila

Most of the major spirits can be made from a variety of source ingredients. Such is not the case with tequila, distilled from primarily blue agave, and made only in Mexico. This specificity lends tequila a collection of stereotypes, most of which are unearned. While cheap mass-produced tequilas can be harsh and unpleasant, there are also exceptional blends and distillations so fine and smooth they are best served straight for sipping.

Whiskey

Much like gin, whiskey is so varied in tone, flavor, ingredients, and profile that it can be hard to know what sort to add to a drink. Speaking most generally, whiskey is a spirit made from fermenting grain mash, generally aged in wooden barrels or casks to develop maturity, color, and flavor. Ever wonder about the difference between whiskey and whisky? Us too. Someone probably answers that in a book somewhere.

Common On-Hand Mixers

Most of the simple mixers you'll want on hand for a cocktail tavern party are self-explanatory. Juices, milk, soft drinks, and the like require little explanation. We'd still provide one for each, but unlike RPG authors we don't get paid by the word, so you figure those mixers out. Following is a guide to basic syrups that can be easily made at home, as well as a few of the more esoteric ingredients found in this book.

Simple Syrup

This common mix-in couldn't be easier to get set up in your home bar tool kit. It's just equal parts granulated sugar and water, simmered and stirred until the sugar is dissolved, and then stored in the refrigerator until it's called for. That's it. That's the entire recipe.

> **Complex Syrup**
>
> This exceptionally difficult to manufacture fluid is also famously challenging to imbibe and digest. No recipes in this book call for it, and we've never seen it required elsewhere. However, the existence of simple syrup suggests that it must exist, and it is therefore included for the sake of completion, as most nerd things are.

Honey Syrup

Honey can be difficult to utilize in cocktail construction, since it will harden in cold water and not mix well no matter how much you stir it. A shame, since honey can lend a variety of floral and earthy sweet flavors to cocktails. There's a solution though, quite literally.

Just combine a cup of honey and a half cup of warm water in your squeeze bottle of choice and give the whole thing a good shake. This flavorful concoction will keep for weeks on the counter or in the refrigerator. It also works with flavored honeys. You'll find a few recipes in this book that call for either honey syrup or spicy hot honey syrup.

Sweet and Sour Mix

Yes, you can just buy this in stores. That said, you can also just get cocktails in bars, so let's apply that can-do spirit and make your own delicious sweet and sour mix for a variety of cocktails. It's easy! Just mix equal parts water, sugar, fresh lemon juice, and fresh lime juice. And if you already have simple syrup, just use one part of that instead of the water and sugar. Don't cook this one; just combine, mix, and store for later. Oh, and if you'd like margarita mix, keep the ratio, but don't put in the lemon juice. One part each sugar, water, and lime juice is all you need for classic marg-crafting.

Citric Acid

There are dozens of household uses for this powdered acid product. It can be used for cleaning, as a foaming agent, and in cosmetics and pharmaceuticals. For the purposes of this book, we primarily use it for the chapter on how to chelate limescale off of your hot water heater and associated fixtures. Just kidding! We use it in place of lemon juice in recipes that call for both sourness and clarity. It's readily available in stores and online.

Luster Dust

A tiny amount of this goes a very long way. This is essentially superfine edible glitter that you can mix into drinks to give them a visible "magicky" shimmer effect. You've likely seen it already mixed with some drinks available in stores. It's easy to find in a variety of colors online and in the cake decorating aisle of grocery stores.

Basic Bar Tools You'll Need to Get Started

You'll require a cocktail shaker for most of these cocktails. Bar spoons and measuring spoons or cups that show small ounce amounts would also be exceptionally useful. As for glassware, there are a dazzling, near-infinite array of types of glasses that you can use to serve libations in, from the humble highball to the swoopy Nick and Nora. You don't need to concern yourself too much with having the perfect glass set for every occasion, however, and can do quite well starting out with some shot glasses, some martini glasses, and some tumblers. In each recipe we've made a suggestion of the appropriate glass, but if you don't have it, that's cool as well. Just use what you've got on hand.

All right. Now you know the basics. Let's get mixing, people! Adventuring parties, in search of dragons, are getting thirsty.

Chapter 1

SPIRITED SPECIES

Here you'll discover beverages inspired by orcs, dwarves, elves, and similar denizens of dungeons and drinkeries. Choose wisely, as your selection will impact your attributes (*Düngeonmeister* uses thirteen unique and proprietary attributes, but is first among those in the school of thought that attributes should really be up to the bartender, thus their obvious omission from all future recipes).

Three Halflings in a Trench Coat

Complexity: 1   **Yields 1 cocktail**

It is a well-known fact that there is little more terrifying or confusing than the combined might of three halflings in a trench coat coming right at you. In the same way, the three rums that find themselves hidden in a coat of sweetness and sour juices are sure to be a powerhouse.

1 ounce white rum

1 ounce dark rum

1 ounce demerara rum

¾ ounce lime juice

¾ ounce white grapefruit juice

1 ounce honey syrup (*see recipe in Tavern Basics*)

2 ounces club soda (or enough to fill)

1 orange wheel for garnish

1 skewer for garnish

3 stemmed maraschino cherries

1. Combine rums, juices, and syrup in an ice-filled shaker and shake well to combine and chill.

2. Strain into a Collins glass filled with ice. Fill to top with club soda.

3. Garnish with skewered orange wheel and cherries.

DÜNGEONMEISTER TIP

Originally, there were only two halflings in a trench coat, and it was just so they could get into bars and restricted movies. It wasn't until an enterprising third joined in that the world was to know the true power of a wobbly mass with six arms and a dapper fashion sense.

Dark Elf

Complexity: 1   **Yields 1 cocktail**

Deep in the recesses of the underworld, the shadowy dark elves plot
and conspire in the pitch-dark of the eternal night. Sitting around
plotting in darkness isn't especially sexy, so they often sit at fancy
tables drinking exotic underworld cocktails made from secretive,
maleficent ingredients. Since maleficent ingredients are often not
dolphin-safe or free of GMOs, we've attempted to re-create the
umbral nectars these elves enjoy using simple ingredients.

2 ounces white rum
¾ ounce peach schnapps
3 ounces cherry juice (as dark as
  possible)
2 teaspoons grenadine

2 stemmed and pitted dark
  fresh cherries (such as Bing or
  Sweetheart)
2 stemmed maraschino cherries

1. Combine rum, schnapps, cherry juice, and grenadine in an ice-filled
   shaker.

2. Shake vigorously to mix and chill. Strain into a martini glass.

3. Garnish with a toothpick spear of alternating fresh and maraschino
   cherries.

Gnomish Gnightcap

Complexity: 1   **Yields 1 cocktail**

Gnomes are gnown for having gnightcaps that are gnothing short of mag-nificent. Bitter, sweet, dry, and refreshing all at once, this drink is every bit as complex as any gnomish invention but exceedingly easy to make.

1 ounce London Dry gin
1 ounce Campari
1 ounce sweet vermouth
1 orange twist (peel) for garnish

1. Combine all ingredients except orange twist together in an ice-filled shaker. Shake vigorously to combine and chill.

2. Strain into a tumbler or highball glass over cubed ice.

3. Garnish with orange twist.

DÜNGEONMEISTER TIP

The tradition of ending an evening with a drink is attributed to Delbar Tippletinkler, a hero among the gnomish people. Originally, the drink had a sprinkle of dirt in it as well. Not on purpose. That's just what happens when you make all your drinks in a burrow.

Dwarven Forge

Complexity: 3   **Yields 1 cocktail**

Dwarves are master craftsmen, known far and wide for their attention to detail, resistance to the heat of their mighty furnaces, and mastery over the blend of artistry and function. To pay proper homage to the stout axe-loving folk, this cocktail is a challenge to make and a reward to master. It's also on fire, so be extremely careful and follow all the recommended safety instructions.

For the Spiced Berry Coulis:
12 ounces frozen berry blend
3 sprigs thyme
½ cup granulated sugar
½ cup water
2 drops red food coloring

For the Cocktail:
2 ounces spiced rum
1½ ounces Spiced Berry Coulis
¾ ounce fresh lemon juice
2 teaspoons overproof rum

1. **For the Spiced Berry Coulis:** Combine berries, thyme, sugar, and water in a medium saucepan.

2. Cook over medium heat to boiling, stirring until all sugar has dissolved and the fruit has fully softened, roughly 8 minutes.

3. Remove mixture from the heat, transfer to a medium bowl, and refrigerate until cold, at least 1 hour.

4. Strain mixture through a sieve into a storage bottle (a funnel may help here), then add the drops of food coloring for extra color.

5. Refrigerate until ready to use.

continued on next page

6. **For the Cocktail:** Combine all ingredients except overproof rum in an ice-filled shaker and shake to combine and chill.

7. Strain into a coupe glass, leaving room at the top of the glass.

8. Slowly pour overproof rum over the back of a spoon into the glass to form a layer over top of cocktail (be careful not to fill the glass).

9. Light cocktail with a match and observe. Safety note: Do not move cocktail or consume cocktail while still lit. Do not attempt to blow out a flaming cocktail. To put out, smother the fire with a saucer or cocktail shaker. Do not allow the fire to "burn out," as alcohol fires can be invisible. Always ensure fire is safely out before consuming.

DÜNGEONMEISTER TIP

For maximum Dwarven Forge showiness, wait until this drink is lit and burning, then from a safe distance above the flames, sprinkle a pinch of cinnamon down from above. This will create beautiful forge sparks, which dwarves hold in high esteem (at beard's length, of course).

Aasimartini

Complexity: 1   **Yields 1 cocktail**

A cocktail as holy as drinking can legally be outside of a church or temple, the Aasimartini distills divinity into a delightful package. While the aasimar merely has an angel or two somewhere in the family tree, the Aasimartini delivers glory on high and a pleasant coffee aroma to boot.

2 ounces Irish cream liqueur
1 ounce vodka
1 ounce brewed espresso
1 star fruit slice for garnish

1. Combine all ingredients except garnish in an ice-filled shaker and shake well to combine.

2. Strain into a chilled martini glass.

3. Garnish with star fruit slice.

DÜNGEONMEISTER TIP

Several variations on this cocktail exist, from the Half-Celestial Templarita to the Deva & Coke, but we've elected to include the original, because that's the lawful good thing to do.

Half 'n' Half-Orc

Complexity: 1   **Yields 1 cocktail**

Half-orcs have a hard time fitting into society. They are rejected by their brutal orcish cousins and treated as dangerous criminals and monsters by their human relatives. There is, however, a fierce nobility to these folk, and those that do befriend them are rewarded, in this case by a refreshing blend of mint and cream that's accepted by just about everyone.

1 ounce green crème de menthe
1 ounce crème de cacao
2 ounces half and half

1. Combine all ingredients in an ice-filled shaker and mix gently.

2. Strain into a chilled martini glass.

DÜNGEONMEISTER TIP

The Half 'n' Half-Orc is best garnished with mint leaves, but also commonly with dark chocolate shavings. Learning to trim these shavings with a two-handed greataxe can be rough going at first, but it's a rewarding process you'll learn to appreciate.

Sleep Immunity

Complexity: 1   **Yields 1 cocktail**

Among the many things that elves are known for, perhaps one of the lesser-known qualities is their inherent sleeplessness and inability to be put in magical slumber. With this caffeine concoction, you, too, can feel what it's like to be one of the fair folk, at least for a time.

2 ounces vodka
1 (8-ounce) can energy drink of choice (larger is fine)

1. Pour vodka into a highball glass filled with ice.

2. Top up with energy drink.

DÜNGEONMEISTER TIP

Since its creation, this particular cocktail has been highly popular with those that wish to feel some of the power of elven kind flowing through them. There is a much less popular dwarven drink that lets you detect the slope of a floor—probably because it accomplishes this by being powerful enough to lay you flat out on the ground.

Tiefling's Breakfast

Complexity: 2   **Yields 1 cocktail**

Tieflings tend to eat like they live, with more than a little smoke, fire, and danger. This beverage serves as a brunch time pick-me-up that the fiendish among you can enjoy for its fiery heat and refreshing tang.

3 dashes celery salt, divided
2 lime wedges, divided
1½ ounces bourbon
2 dashes hot sauce
2 dashes Worcestershire sauce

1 teaspoon wasabi
Approximately 2 ounces tomato
 juice to fill
1 celery stalk for garnish, leaves on

1. Fill the bottom of a small bowl with 1 dash celery salt. Rub 1 lime wedge around the rim of a pint glass and coat with celery salt.

2. Fill glass with ice and add 2 dashes of celery salt and all other ingredients except tomato juice, celery stalk, and remaining lime wedge.

3. Fill with tomato juice and stir well.

4. Garnish with celery stalk and lime wedge.

⚔ DÜNGEONMEISTER TIP

This is not the only drink to be named for the tiefling race. In fact, there is one for every meal of the day. The Tiefling's Brunch tends to just be a mixture of champagne and catty gossip.

Slippery Grippli

Complexity: 2   **Yields 1 shot**

If you're looking for green and slippery, you can't go wrong with the tiny batrachian swamp dwellers known as the grippli. Masters of camouflage and ambush, these tiny creatures attack from the shadows in deadly flashes of emerald. To create this cocktail reminiscent of these swamp denizens and their swamp, a layered shooter provides swamp water (the brown of the schnapps), bull rushes (the tan of Irish cream), and frog-fellow (sweet melon liqueur), all in one candy-sweet shot.

½ ounce butterscotch schnapps
¼ ounce Irish cream liqueur
½ ounce melon liqueur

1. Pour butterscotch schnapps into a shot glass.

2. Carefully pour cream over the back of a spoon so it goes into the glass more slowly, creating a layer of cream over schnapps.

3. Repeat step 2 using melon liqueur.

DÜNGEONMEISTER TIP

Applying any garnishes here would really be gilding the foxtail. Honestly, that's probably for the best, as the original garnish suggestions in the guidebook were two isopods on a toothpick and a hellgrammite at the bottom.

Chapter 2

CLASS-Y DRINKS

Looking to drink a cut above the rabble? Try mixing up a round of these character classics and share them around the table. Most folks are stuck with common drinks, but you've got a backstory, specialized training, and maybe even a familiar! With these libations, you're all set to start gaining levels. Or even to multiclass (multiclass only in moderation).

Barbarian Rage

Complexity: 1

Yields 1 cocktail

Regardless of their homeland or upbringing, one thing all barbarian warriors have in common is the ability to call upon a seemingly inhuman rage while in combat. With this combination of spirits and energy drink, you, too, can feel what it's like to be all brawn and no brains.

1 ounce spiced rum

1 ounce Amaretto

1 ounce tequila

1 ounce vodka

1 ounce gin

1 ounce blue curaçao

1 ounce light rum

1 ounce black raspberry liqueur

1 ounce melon liqueur

1 ounce coconut rum

1 (8-ounce) can energy drink of choice (or larger)

1. Combine all ingredients except energy drink in a shaker with cracked ice, then shake and pour into a pint glass or large mug.

2. Fill with energy drink.

DÜNGEONMEISTER TIP

In a pinch, the cocktail glass can be replaced with the skull of a recently defeated foe. Be aware that this drink will cause you to fly into an energy-fueled mania of bad decisions where you may not be able to tell friend from foe. Before going into another rage, take a short rest.

Bard's Songs

Complexity: 1   **Yields 6 cocktails**

When adventuring in the wilds or relaxing in a tavern, nothing can soothe the frayed nerves of a wanderer quite like a song from a bard. This drink has all the sparkle and glamor of the best showmen out there and is just as refreshing as kicking your feet up and listening to a great tune.

8 ounces Pimm's No. 1 Cup
4 ounces gin
2 tablespoons lemon juice
2 tablespoons grenadine
32 ounces sparkling wine
1 cup raspberries for garnish

1. Combine Pimm's No. 1 Cup, gin, lemon juice, and grenadine in an ice filled pitcher, and stir to combine

2. Strain equally into six chilled wine flutes. Fill each glass with equal amounts sparkling wine and raspberries.

DÜNGEONMEISTER TIP

One of the great arguments among the magic users of the world is whether a bard's song is actually magic or if they've somehow found a way to inspire through music in a way that seems magical. However, I once saw a bard get an ogre to dance a waltz with a halfling, so I'm going to say magic.

Flavored Enemy

Complexity: 1   **Yields 1 cocktail**

The rangers that wander the wilderness are known to have specific enemies that they come to study and know in great detail. These enemies come in many different flavors, and this is just one flavor that you can master.

1½ ounces vanilla vodka
3 ounces orange juice
Splash cranberry juice
1 orange wheel for garnish

1. Add vodka and juices to an ice-filled highball glass and stir well.

2. Garnish with orange wheel.

DÜNGEONMEISTER TIP

The tradition among rangers to focus on a single type of enemy has a long and storied history to it. You see, one day, a ranger got really lazy and decided to say that he only fought goblinoids so the local town would leave him alone about the giants who were roaming around.

Holy Water

Complexity: 1   **Yields 1 cocktail**

Holy water, when flung on a vampire or other intelligent undead, will repulse the creature and burn its vile hide as it shrinks away from the wielder. That said, actual holy water tastes like water, so it makes a lot of sense to hurl it at itinerant Draculas. This floral twist on the classic margarita tastes holy, so you may wish to retain it for consumption instead.

2 ounces reposado tequila
1 ounce elderflower liqueur
1 ounce fresh-squeezed lime juice
1 lime wheel for garnish

1. Combine all ingredients except lime wheel in an ice-filled shaker and shake vigorously to combine and chill.

2. Strain and serve in an iced cocktail glass.

3. Garnish with lime wheel.

DÜNGEONMEISTER TIP

Warning note: Hurling this drink at a vampire will render his waistcoat and silly red cloak all sticky in the few seconds before he murders you, so consider offering him a glass, instead.

Necromancer

Complexity: 1   **Yields 1 cocktail**

The art of necromancy has often been looked down on as evil and unnatural. While this drink may seem to be as cloudy as the eyes of a newly risen corpse, it has a perfectly balanced flavor with citrusy strength.

1 ounce gin
1 ounce Cointreau
1 ounce Lillet Blanc
1 ounce lemon juice
Dash absinthe
1 orange twist (peel) for garnish

1. Combine all ingredients except orange twist in an ice-filled shaker and shake vigorously to combine and chill.

2. Strain into a chilled coupe glass.

3. Garnish with orange twist.

DÜNGEONMEISTER TIP

Necromancers get a bad rap, and I can understand where most people are coming from. But, for us, there's honestly no one else we would rather turn to when we need some body.

Sneak Attack

Complexity: 2   **Yields 1 cocktail**

Rogues are known for being able to sneak up on the unsuspecting and take them out with one go. This is also true for this deceptively strong drink that masks its power in sweet and refreshing flavors.

2 ounces white rum
¾ ounce Cointreau
1¼ ounces Luxardo or other maraschino liqueur
¾ ounce lime juice
¼ ounce simple syrup (*see recipe in Tavern Basics*)
½ cup crushed ice

1. Pour all ingredients into a blender.

2. Blend on the pulse setting until smooth.

3. Pour into a chilled coupe glass.

DÜNGEONMEISTER TIP

This drink used to be known as The Backstabber and was much more difficult to make. Over the years, more enlightened bartenders have made variations of it so that it is much more accessible if maybe less crushingly powerful. Some people still mistakenly call it the wrong name.

Stunning Smite

Complexity: 2   **Yields 1 cocktail**

Paladins can call upon their deity to help them smite evil and leave their foes stunned and reeling. This drink will smite what ails you as the warmth and sweetness spread, leaving all those you serve stunned by how good it is.

For the Cinnamon Cider:
½ cup apple cider
4 cinnamon sticks, divided

For the Cocktail:
1 ounce whiskey
½ ounce lemon juice
Splash maple syrup
3 apple slices for garnish

1. **For the Cinnamon Cider:** Combine apple cider and 3 cinnamon sticks in a small saucepan and cook over medium heat until simmering, about 3 minutes.

2. Turn off the heat and let mixture cool to room temperature.

3. **For the Cocktail:** Combine Cinnamon Cider, whiskey, lemon juice, and syrup in an ice-filled shaker and shake to combine.

4. Strain into a tumbler filled with ice.

5. Garnish with apple slices and remaining cinnamon stick.

Sweet and Sour-cerer

Complexity: 1   **Yields 1 cocktail**

The sorcerer is a being of contrasts. They are bestowed with great power and yet have not learned how to properly use it. They are both human and yet something else. In the same way, this cocktail blends both sour and sweet into a drink that is more than it seems.

1 cup sweet and sour mix
$^1/_3$ cup cherry liqueur
$^1/_3$ cup white rum
1 lime wheel for garnish

1. Combine all ingredients except lime wheel in an ice-filled shaker and shake to combine.

2. Strain cocktail into an ice-filled tumbler.

3. Garnish with lime wheel.

DÜNGEONMEISTER TIP

"Sorcerers will try to tell you that they don't actually have any dragons in their ancestry and that it's actually just their inherent power. They are liars. Everyone knows that you only get magic powers without studying if your parents slept around with giant lizards." —A wizard

Sword and Chambord

Complexity: 1   **Yields 1 cocktail**

In the wilds of the land, there is little that a warrior can count on aside
from their own strength and the weapons they wield. You have to make
sure everything is perfectly balanced so that nothing fails you at the worst
moment. This drink manages to strike that perfect balance of spicy, sweet,
and strong that will leave you refreshed and ready for anything.

2 ounces vodka
½ ounce black raspberry liqueur
½ ounce lime juice
4 ounces ginger beer
1 lime wheel for garnish
5 fresh raspberries for garnish

1. Combine vodka, black raspberry liqueur, and lime juice in an ice-filled
   Moscow mule mug.

2. Top the mug with ginger beer.

3. Garnish with lime wheel and raspberries scattered across the drink
   surface.

DÜNGEONMEISTER TIP

Those discerning drinkers who favor the taste of the Sword and
Chambord cocktail will often have similar ideas on how it should be
presented. Specifically, it is determined to be best when served in
a tankard.

Chapter 3

SKILLED SELECTIONS

Dazzle your friends with a range of skillful cocktails. You can also use your mastery over these arts to embarrass your foes, since noncombat is the best way to avoid a fight. There's nothing secondary about our skills, so you can rest assured they're guaranteed to work. If you make your roll, anyway.

Healing Surge

Complexity: 1

Here's a blast of refreshing energy, a cool breeze that soothes the burn, and the pick-me-up you were looking for. This sour-sweet elixir will cure what ails you (please note that depending on the spell level of the user, this might only cure specifically any thirst that ails you).

1½ ounces tequila
1½ ounces sour apple liqueur
1 ounce lime juice
½ ounce simple syrup (*see recipe in Tavern Basics*)
1 slice Granny Smith apple for garnish
4–6 ounces lemon-lime soda

1. Combine all ingredients except apple slice and soda in an ice-filled shaker and shake vigorously to combine.

2. Fill a cocktail glass with ice and add apple slice.

3. Strain the cocktail into the glass, then fill with soda.

4. Garnish with apple slice.

DÜNGEONMEISTER TIP

The best thing about this beverage is that consuming it is only a minor action, leaving you free to attack and move this round. Please only attack in moderation.

Escape Artist

Complexity: 1   **Yields 1 cocktail**

Rogues are often possessed of a slippery talent to loose their bonds and break their chains, sneaking free to pick pockets and find and remove traps again. To commemorate and encapsulate their greasy greatness, try the Escape Artist, a fresh, bright, herbaceous martini well lubricated with olive oil and vodka to keep things loose and law-scoffing.

1 lemon wedge with peel
4 fresh basil leaves
4 ounces vodka
½ ounce simple syrup (see recipe in Tavern Basics)
½ ounce plus drizzle extra-virgin olive oil, divided
½ ounce dry vermouth
1 lemon twist (peel) for garnish

1. Muddle lemon and basil leaves in the bottom of a mixing glass.

2. Add several ice cubes, vodka, syrup, ½ ounce olive oil, and vermouth to glass. Swirl to combine for 30 seconds.

3. Strain into a chilled martini glass.

4. Drizzle remaining olive oil on top to form a small pool. Garnish with lemon twist.

Point Blank Shot

Complexity: 1   **Yields 1 shot**

It takes a strong will as an archer to be able to remain cool and collected when someone comes running up to you with their sword out. Taking this shot will also require a steady hand and an open mind, as these two liquors combine into an entirely new flavor.

1½ ounces gin
¾ ounce whiskey
1 lemon twist (peel) for garnish

1. Combine gin and whiskey in an ice-filled shaker and shake vigorously to combine.

2. Strain into a shot glass.

3. Squeeze lemon twist over the shot and hang on the rim as a garnish.

DÜNGEONMEISTER TIP

There was a variation of this drink that was far less popular known as the Far Shot. It involved trying to throw a shot into a friend's mouth, and after many painful eye accidents, it was abandoned.

Seduction Rolls

Complexity: 2   **Yields 8 cocktails**

The art of seduction is a curious thing. There is no single thing that can make one seductive; it is a blend of many different factors. With all the different parts mixed together here, you get one singularly enticing drink that is sweet and tangy and leaves you wanting more.

16 ounces cranberry juice
8 ounces vodka
4 ounces Amaretto
3 tablespoons fresh orange juice
2 tangerines, cut into 16 sections for garnish

1. Mix cranberry juice, vodka, Amaretto, and orange juice in a pitcher.

2. Cover and chill until ready to serve.

3. Add 1 cup of mixture to an ice-filled shaker and shake vigorously.

4. Strain into two martini glasses and garnish each glass with 2 tangerine sections. Repeat three more times.

DÜNGEONMEISTER TIP

A Seduction Roll is romantic enough to have a chance to work on anyone. The nice thing is, with eight different chances, you're even more likely to find someone that thinks you're as special as your mother always tells everyone.

Power Attack

Complexity: 1   **Yields 1 cocktail**

When fighting an enemy with more meat than brains, you sometimes need to sacrifice a little finesse for a little more raw power. While this drink seems sweet, fruity, and a little tart, it's packing a heck of a punch.

1 ounce Southern Comfort (you could substitute any good bourbon here, though be forewarned, this will pump up the alcohol kick)
½ ounce vanilla vodka
½ ounce sloe gin

½ ounce Cointreau
½ ounce Amaretto
½ ounce lemon juice
4 ounces orange juice
1 orange wedge for garnish

1. Combine all ingredients except orange juice and orange wedge in an ice-filled shaker and shake vigorously to combine.

2. Strain into an ice-filled cocktail glass.

3. Fill with orange juice, and garnish with orange wedge.

DÜNGEONMEISTER TIP

You don't always have to swing as hard as you can. Sometimes, it's not right to do so. Sometimes you've got to line up a shot and get in flanking position. Sometimes you've got to wait. Sometimes you've got to swing late. Sometimes you've got to say, "Hey, I'm gonna smack you, softly."

Royal Diplomacy

Complexity: 1   **Yields 1 cocktail**

In the courts and noble houses of the world, sometimes diplomacy can use a little bit of social lubrication to get the proceedings started. This deceivingly sweet drink can sneak up on you just like the best courtesan.

½ ounce Southern Comfort
½ ounce blended whiskey (such as Crown Royal)
½ ounce Amaretto
½ ounce orange juice
½ ounce pineapple juice
½ ounce cranberry juice
Splash grenadine
1 orange wheel for garnish

1. Combine all ingredients except orange wheel in an ice filled shaker and shake vigorously to combine.

2. Strain into a cocktail glass filled with ice.

3. Garnish with orange wheel.

DÜNGEONMEISTER TIP

It's often asked what the difference between standard diplomacy and royal diplomacy is. If you're being calm and gracious in order to get everyone to agree, that's regular diplomacy. If you're being calm and gracious in order to not get beheaded, that's royal diplomacy.

Stealth Checks

Complexity: 2

These innocuous shots may look like little more than clear, firm gin and tonics, and in fact they are just that. However, should they fall victim to the directed attention of a UV spot check, they'll light up as bright as a rogue who should never have split the party. The secret? Quinine in the tonic water reacts to ultraviolet light in spectacular fluorescence.

1 cup plus 2 tablespoons tonic water

1 (¼-ounce) envelope unflavored powdered gelatin

2 tablespoons granulated sugar

6 ounces gin

1 tablespoon freshly squeezed lime juice

1 tablespoon rose water

1. In a small saucepan over medium heat, bring tonic water to a boil.

2. Place gelatin and sugar in a medium heatproof bowl, then add boiled tonic water.

3. Stir until completely dissolved, then set aside 10 minutes or until cooled to room temperature.

4. Stir in gin, lime juice, and rose water.

5. Divide the mixture equally into shot glasses (approximately ten US glasses).

6. Refrigerate until set firm, at least 2 hours.

7. Serve, using any sort of black light to create the glow effect. This will work best in an otherwise dark room.

Turn Undead

Complexity: 1 **Yields 1 cocktail**

When the dead rise up and threaten the living, it is the holy clerics that can stem the tide and cast back the horde. With this drink, you will find that the bitter and sour that you might expect is turned into something much more pleasing.

1 ounce vodka
1 ounce coffee liqueur
2 teaspoons fresh lemon juice

1. Pour all ingredients over ice in an old-fashioned glass.

2. Stir and serve.

DÜNGEONMEISTER TIP

There has been some confusion over the ability of Turn Undead. Often an embarrassed cleric or paladin will have to calmly explain that it is not, in fact, a way to join the ranks of the unliving. If one wishes to turn undead, it's probably wise to seek out a necromancer instead.

Twin Strikes

Complexity: 1   **Yields 2 shots**

When you want to ensure that your foes will not escape unscathed, it's best to make sure your shot counts by coming at them from multiple angles. This simple and effective shot comes at you with a sweetness from the liqueur and then follows up with the tartness of the lime.

1½ ounces vodka
¾ ounce triple sec
¾ ounce lime juice

1. Combine all ingredients in an ice-filled shaker and shake vigorously to combine.

2. Strain into two shot glasses.

DÜNGEONMEISTER TIP

Many rangers practice to become ambidextrous so that they can dual wield with much more efficiency. This becomes an even more practical skill when attempting to get multiple drinks from the bar... to share with the party, of course.

Chapter 4

MAGIC MIXERS

You can have a little bit of magic right in your own home with these drinks straight out of a very drunken wizard's spell book. We've supplied the lists for all the material components you'll need to get started. The somatic component is drinking them, and the verbal component is going "Wooo!" while you do so.

Acid Arrow

Complexity: 1   **Yields 1 shot**

There's something magical about this fruity and sweet blend of ingredients. Once mixed together, the herbal top helps to counter the spell of overwhelming sugar in the juice.

½ ounce coconut rum
¾ ounce pineapple juice
¼ ounce Jägermeister

1. Combine coconut rum and pineapple juice in a shaker with ice and shake well.

2. Strain into a shot glass.

3. Float Jägermeister on top by pouring it slowly over the back of a spoon into the glass to form a layer.

4. If you want to "upcast" this shot into a cocktail, make the ingredients 1 ounce each, add to an ice-filled shaker to combine and chill, and strain into an ice-filled tumbler.

DÜNGEONMEISTER TIP

This shot to the head is certain to do some acidic damage. Just make sure your aim is correct when you let this one loose, or you could be dealing with some splash damage.

Coors Light Wounds

Complexity: 2   **Yields 2 cocktails**

Even after a long rest and a good night's sleep, sometimes there are ailments that linger on. Should you find yourself in greatest need, you can always petition the local cleric to lift your spirits and repair your aches and complaints through divine magic. Or, barring access to divine casters, you can try this smoky, spiced delight.

2 tablespoons kosher or sea salt

Tajín or other chili spice blend

½ teaspoon honey

2 ounces tomato juice

1 tablespoon fresh lime juice

12 ounces Coors Light or other beer

1½ teaspoons chipotle hot sauce

1 teaspoon Worcestershire sauce

Dash soy sauce

1. Mix salt and chili spices to cover the bottom of a small dish. Dip the rims of two rocks glasses in honey, then dip in the salt mixture to coat. Fill both glasses with ice.

2. In a pitcher, combine tomato juice and lime juice, beer, hot sauce, Worcestershire sauce, and soy sauce. Stir to mix.

3. Pour into prepared glasses.

DÜNGEONMEISTER TIP

This concoction is rumored to ease your passage from even the most harrowing hangover. If you don't have any Coors Light on hand, congratulations! Give yourself 250 XP for not being burdened with cheap American lager. Now just substitute a tasty amber Mexican beer like a Dos Equis Ambar or a Modelo Negra.

Elemental Plane of Fire

Complexity: 2   **Yields 1 punch bowl (serves about 32)**

On the Plane of Fire, there is no escape from the intense heat and the flames that threaten to consume everything. While not quite as inescapable as its namesake, the Elemental Plane of Fire will give you a spicy kick while still delivering a tangy, tasty treat.

1 small seedless watermelon (about 5 pounds), peeled and cubed
2 cups sparkling water
2 jalapeños
8 ounces lime juice
16 ounces tequila
$^1/_3$ cup granulated sugar
1 tablespoon Tajín or other spice blend
1 tablespoon salt
4 lime wedges for garnish

1. Combine watermelon and sparkling water in a blender and blend until smooth, approximately 30–45 seconds.

2. Strain pulp through a sieve into a punch bowl.

3. Chop jalapeños into coins and shake loose excess seeds.

4. Add lime juice, tequila, sugar, and jalapeño slices to bowl and stir.

5. Chill until ready to serve.

6. Combine spice blend with salt in a small bowl. Run a lime wedge around the rim of several punch glasses and dip the rims into the spice and salt blend.

7. Pour beverage into prepared glasses with ice and serve.

Black Mana

Complexity: 2   **Yields 1 cocktail**

Seeking something a little sinister? Try out a Black Mana, the coalesced essence of death, decay, and subversion. Sure, that might not sound like an appetizing start to a cocktail, but good news abounds, because the denizens of eternal night like coffee drinks as much as we do, if not more. This sweet midnight draft will keep you going through hours of grave-bound machinations.

3 ounces vanilla vodka
1 ounce coffee liqueur
1 ounce crème de cacao
1 ounce chilled espresso
½ teaspoon powdered activated charcoal

1. Combine vodka, coffee liqueur, and crème de cacao in a shaker with ice and shake to combine.

2. Strain into a chilled martini glass.

3. Add chilled espresso and powdered activated charcoal and stir.

Green Mana

Complexity: 1

Yields 1 cocktail

The magical influences of wild places, the spiritual energy that lives in leaf, soil, and creature alike…green mana is nature made manifest. To appreciate the best it has to offer, try this enchanting blend of melon, mint, and lime, which will set your mind to all things natural and your soul to birdsong.

15 mint leaves, divided
¾ ounce melon liqueur
¾ ounce fresh lime juice
1½ ounces white rum
2 ounces club soda

1. Add 10 mint leaves and melon liqueur to a shaker and muddle.

2. Combine with lime juice, rum, and ice and shake to chill.

3. Strain into a rocks glass filled with ice.

4. Add club soda and stir.

5. Garnish with remaining mint leaves.

DÜNGEONMEISTER TIP

The original version of this cocktail also contained 2 tablespoons of assorted spider parts and most of an ape. We've modified the beverage into a vegetarian blend out of respect for nature (and because the apes kept eating the good spider parts).

Faerie Fire

Complexity: 2

Yields 1 cocktail

Sparks and glitter in the darkness of the swamp portend mischievous ghosts, protective nature spirits, or secretive druids conducting ancient rituals. In this orange-essence blue beverage, they merely portend the presence of sparkling LED ice cubes.

2 ounces blue curaçao
1½ ounces gin
1 ounce sweet vermouth
½ ounce orange juice
1–2 LED flashing ice cubes
1 orange wheel for garnish

1. Combine all ingredients except LED ice cubes and orange wheel in a shaker with ice and shake well.

2. Pour into a hurricane glass with LED ice cubes inside.

3. Garnish with orange wheel on top.

DÜNGEONMEISTER TIP

There are a variety of ways to acquire glowing, blinking ice cubes. You can seek the services of friendly enchanters, trap the spirit of a lantern ghost on a midwinter's night, or—by far the most common—get them online, since they generally run a dozen for about $15.

Hpnotiq Pattern

Complexity: 1   **Yields 1 cocktail**

A clever mage knows that you don't have to kill your opponent when you can much more easily dazzle them with a swirling, colorful display. When these two liquids mix, you get a lustrous, swirling, color-changing concoction that has a fruity and unique flavor.

3 ounces crushed ice
1 ounce Hpnotiq or other lustrous swirling liqueur
1 ounce cognac

1. Place ice in a cocktail glass.

2. Pour Hpnotiq first and then cognac over ice.

3. Stir to combine.

DÜNGEONMEISTER TIP

The interesting thing about a spell that mesmerizes all who look at it is that nobody can really remember what the pattern in question actually looks like. There have been varying loose accounts with some saying it looked like a human infant that was dancing and others saying the pattern took the form of a clothed feline playing some manner of keyed instrument.

Blue Mana

Complexity: 1   **Yields 1 cocktail**

The fury of the seas, the rush of the breeze, and the quiet contemplation of the scholar all embody the complexity of blue mana. So, too, can this combination of sweet, sour, and bitter be swirled together into a concoction that is bound to be an inspiration.

1 lime wedge
2 tablespoons coarse or granulated sugar
2 ounces cranberry juice
1 ounce vodka or citrus vodka

1 ounce blue curaçao
½ ounce fresh lime juice
Pinch (approximately ½ teaspoon) pearl luster dust

1. Rub lime wedge around the rim of a rocks glass. Sprinkle sugar onto a small plate, then dip the moistened rim into the sugar to coat lightly.

2. Combine all remaining ingredients except luster dust in a shaker with ice and shake to combine.

3. Strain into sugared glass. Sprinkle luster dust over finished cocktail and serve.

DÜNGEONMEISTER TIP

Mages who favor the use of blue mana are famous (or perhaps infamous) for their reliance upon countermagic. It is said that you can always tell when two great blue wizards are dueling by the lack of anything happening.

Red Mana

Complexity: 1   **Yields 1 cocktail**

When you consider a cocktail on the basis of destructive fury, flame, and stone, and aggressive creatures of mountain and warren, whiskey immediately comes to mind. A fiery blend that soothes as it burns, the Red Mana is a challenging drink that you should tap into. For one damage.

2 ounces cinnamon whiskey
2 ounces apple whiskey
1 bar spoon grenadine
2 ounces club soda
1 Thai chili or jalapeño coin for garnish

1. Combine both whiskeys and grenadine in a shaker with ice and shake to chill.

2. Strain into a cocktail glass filled with ice.

3. Add club soda and stir to combine.

4. Garnish with your chosen pepper.

DÜNGEONMEISTER TIP

Many times a goblin raiding party has made its way into the lands of man and caused swaths of destruction. Nobody is sure what spurs the goblins to do this, but the most credible idea postulated so far is that it's the result of drunken dares taken entirely too far.

Goodberries

Complexity: 2   **Yields 4 cocktails**

The druids of the wild lands know that sometimes food is scarce. When needed, they can magically contain an entire meal's worth of nutrition within a single berry. With a little of your own magical know-how, you, too, can create something that packs far more than it seems into one drink. With all the flavor of the sweet berries and a little tartness for balance, you've packed a whole lot of flavor into one glass.

For the Goodberry Syrup:
1 cup water
¾ cup granulated sugar
1 cup frozen mixed berries (blackberries, hulled strawberries,
   blueberries, raspberries, and pitted
   cherries will all work here)

For the Cocktail:
¼ cup superfine sugar
½ cup Goodberry Syrup
4 ounces fresh lime juice
8 ounces blanco tequila
1 skewer for garnish
Assorted fresh berries for garnish
4 lime wheels for garnish

1. **For the Goodberry Syrup:** Combine all ingredients in a medium saucepan over medium heat and bring mixture to a simmer.

2. Cook 4–5 minutes until berries have softened and released their juices and sugar has dissolved.

3. Remove syrup from heat and allow to cool completely, approximately 5–10 minutes.

4. Strain through a mesh sieve to remove berry pieces and set aside.

5. **For the Cocktail:** Put sugar in a small bowl. Moisten the rims of four cocktail glasses with water, then dip the rims into the sugar.

6. Combine Goodberry Syrup, lime juice, and tequila with ice in a shaker and shake until chilled.

7. Strain into cocktail glasses filled with ice.

8. Garnish each glass with skewered berries and lime wheels.

DÜNGEONMEISTER TIP

Philosophers have long wondered what it means to be good. If a berry can be said to be good, then should we not also be? Does the existence of a Goodberry necessitate the hidden threat of the Evilberry? Druids have much to ponder while talking to trees and turning into badgers.

White Mana

Complexity: 1   **Yields 2 cocktails**

White mana is the essence of purity, civilization, and teamwork (which is of course why this recipe makes two servings). Naturally, these things, when distilled and combined into a beverage, will taste like upscale party-friendly chocolate milk. Offer this sweet celebratory drink to the angel in your life.

2 tablespoons granulated sugar
8 ounces chocolate vodka
½ cup sweetened condensed milk

1. In a shallow dish, add enough sugar to coat the bottom. Dip the rims of two martini glasses in water, then dip in the sugar to coat.

2. Combine vodka and condensed milk in a shaker with ice and shake vigorously to combine.

3. Strain into sugared glasses.

> **DÜNGEONMEISTER TIP**
>
> For additional White Mana perfection, allow us to offer a serving suggestion. This drink pairs well with at least fifteen little cocktail weenies.

Magic Mistletoe

Complexity: 2   **Yields 1 cocktail**

Even in a world of magic and monsters, it's still nice to be able to celebrate a holiday with those you love, and appreciate the flavors and smells of winter. With a little mixology magic, you can create a drink that will give the gift of smiles and look good doing it.

Approximately 15 fresh cranberries, divided
2 orange half-wheels
2 ounces London Dry gin
1 ounce simple syrup (see recipe in Tavern Basics)
1 LED flashing ice cube
3 ounces cranberry juice
1½ ounces club soda
1 thyme sprig

1. Muddle 7 cranberries and orange half-wheels in a Collins glass.

2. Add gin and simple syrup, and fill the glass with ice, including LED cube.

3. Fill with cranberry juice and club soda.

4. Stir with thyme sprig, and garnish with remaining cranberries.

DÜNGEONMEISTER TIP

Nobody can quite remember why it is that mistletoe became a traditional decoration in the winter months. Wizards have said that it may have been part of an ancient spell component ritual that would help attack the darkness in the long winter nights.

Psionic Blasts

Complexity: 2   **Yields 6 shots**

A ripping blast of raw mental energy, the psionic blast is the mind mage's most overwhelming and powerful attack. These shots maintain the crackling halo of a psionic at full force, while thoughtfully reducing the mental damage by several orders of magnitude.

2 tablespoons vanilla frosting
Pop Rocks or other popping candy
3 ounces vodka
3 ounces blue curaçao
3 ounces lime juice

1. Add vanilla frosting to a small bowl, then dip the rims of six shot glasses into frosting.

2. Pour candy into a small bowl, then drip frosting-rimmed shot glasses in candy to coat.

3. Combine vodka, blue curaçao, and lime juice with ice in a shaker and shake to chill.

4. Strain into shot glasses.

DÜNGEONMEISTER TIP

If you find your intellect fortress assailed by these libations, consider switching to water for the duration of the evening. Your memories will both remain and thank you in the morning.

Chapter 5

MUDDLED MINIONS

These threats may be diminutive, but they certainly aren't minor. Inspired by the dungeon denizens that are down there in the dark putting in the hard days to make delves scary for adventurers, each of these cocktails packs a punch that's well above its weight class—or its challenge rating, for that matter.

Gelatinous Cubes

Complexity: 2   **Yields 10 gelatin shots**

The translucent dungeon abomination known as the gelatinous cube is famous for deceiving adventurers into ignoring it until it's too late. Then, of course, it dissolves them into a thin nutrient paste. These adorable cinnamon shots can also sneak up on you, so "consume mindlessly," in moderation.

2 cups cold water, divided
4 (¼-ounce) envelopes unflavored gelatin

2 cups granulated sugar
16 ounces cold Goldschläger
1–3 drops green food coloring

1. Place ¼ cup water into a small bowl and empty gelatin packets into water to bloom.

2. In a small saucepan over medium heat, combine sugar and remaining 1¾ cups water.

3. Bring to a simmer and swirl pan until sugar is completely dissolved (do not stir, just swirl the pan).

4. Combine sugar water, bloomed gelatin, and Goldschläger in a medium baking dish and stir to combine.

5. Add as much green food coloring as desired to create slime appearance.

6. Stir again to agitate gold flakes.

7. Chill for at least 2 hours or until fully set.

8. Slice and serve in ten cubes.

Giant Bee

Complexity: 1　　　　　　　　　　　　　　**Yields 1 cocktail**

Sometimes the deadliest monsters make the most delightful drinks. The Giant Bee is a charmingly packaged delivery mechanism for the complexities of good gin and the subtle toothsome sweetness of honey, but beware; it packs a citrusy sting. It may be a random encounter the first time, but after a few sips, you'll want this beverage as a familiar.

2 ounces gin
¾ ounce honey syrup (*see recipe in Tavern Basics*)
1 ounce fresh lemon juice

1. Combine all ingredients in a shaker with ice and shake vigorously to combine.

2. Strain into a rocks glass

DÜNGEONMEISTER TIP

If the Giant Bee proves insufficient as a challenge to your party, consider the following template to give it more body, power, bite, and hit points as needed.

- The Dire Bee: Substitute hot honey syrup for honey syrup.

Goblin Grenades

Complexity: 2   **Yields 12 shots**

These evil green little monsters are anything but subtle. A zesty-sweet combination of jalapeño and strawberry, each shot has a spicy zing to it that you might find delightful until it blows up like the ramshackle concoction it is. For maximum chaos, this beverage is served directly in a jalapeño, rimmed with extra spice for extra pain. And just like the genuine goblinoid article, these little sneaks travel in numbers.

For the Shot Glasses:
12 jalapeños
2 tablespoons Tajín or other spice
  blend
Juice of half of 1 lime

For the Cocktail:
1 lime
2 cups hulled and sliced strawberries
¼ cup granulated sugar
¼ cup water
1 jalapeño, seeded and sliced
2 ounces lemon vodka

1. **For the Shot Glasses:** Cut the tops off the jalapeños and use a spoon or knife to remove seeds and whites from inside.

2. Add spice blend to cover the bottom of a small bowl.

3. Dip each jalapeño in lime juice, then dip in spice blend to rim the jalapeño.

4. Set aside to dry.

5. **For the Cocktail:** Zest and juice the lime.

6. In a medium saucepan over medium heat, combine lime juice, zest, strawberries, sugar, water, and jalapeño and cook for 5 minutes.

7. Transfer to a blender and pulse once.

8. Strain mixture through a fine-mesh sieve.

9. Add vodka to strained mixture and chill in the refrigerator until ready to serve.

10. Pour mixture into each jalapeño immediately before serving.

DÜNGEONMEISTER TIP

Consider placing each jalapeño inside a convenient shot glass that you could have just used in the first place. A great way to serve them is to fill a bowl with little chocolate candies and stand each loaded jalapeño shooter upright among them. Just keep a sharp eye out, as any halfway competent goblin will steal your candies, your bowl, and probably blow up your dog on the way out.

Illithid Substance

Complexity: 2   **Yields 1 cocktail**

Mind flayers are utterly and terrifyingly inhuman, and so are their bars. There's loose brain matter slopping out of highball glasses everywhere; the lighting is dim to the point of near darkness, only occasionally punctuated by mind-addling strobe flashes from nowhere; and the jukebox selection is all Counting Crows B-sides. Of course there are good reasons to visit too, among them this apple and whiskey concoction, which is sour, sweet, and swirling with psychic residue.

2 ounces Irish whiskey
1½ ounces sour apple liqueur
½ ounce lemon juice
½ ounce simple syrup (*see recipe in Tavern Basics*)
¼ teaspoon gold luster dust
1 swizzle stick for garnish

1. Combine all ingredients except swizzle stick in an ice-filled shaker and shake vigorously to combine.

2. Strain into a cocktail glass and garnish with swizzle stick or other stirrer.

DÜNGEONMEISTER TIP

Like virtually every other object or substance dreamed up or concocted by a mind flayer, this beverage was not meant to last in our reality for long. The luster within it will rapidly settle to the bottom in a puddle of silty dust without regular agitation.

1d3 Wandering Minstrels

Complexity: 1   **Yields 1 shot**

If you've gone wandering through the countryside, then you know how inevitable it is that you will eventually run into one to three wandering minstrels when you least expect it. So, too, can this drink blindside you when three different whiskeys all blend together in one place. Enjoy, as much as anyone can enjoy wandering minstrels.

½ ounce Scotch whisky
½ ounce Tennessee whiskey
½ ounce bourbon

1. Combine all ingredients in an ice-filled shaker and shake vigorously to combine and chill.

2. Strain into a shot glass.

DÜNGEONMEISTER TIP

Of course I hear you say, "But it's 1d3 Wandering Minstrels! Why does it always have 3?!" Far be it from us to tell you how to enjoy your whiskey. If you want, roll a d3 and then reduce the different alcohols accordingly.

Kobold Fashioned

Complexity: 1   **Yields 1 cocktail**

The yapping, snapping, and trap-making of the common kobold can be infuriating to those who are forced to live near them, especially the dragons they tend to live in service of. Those dragons need a libation to take their mind off the latest round of some minor clan chieftain inventing the "skunk on a pole" or some similar act of tomfoolery. Such dragons can at least count on kobold bar chiefs, who may only know how to make one cocktail, but it's a trusted classic.

1 sugar cube
2 dashes aromatic bitters
1 or 2 tablespoons plain water
1½ ounces rye whiskey

1 lime twist (peel) for garnish
1 stemmed maraschino cherry for
  garnish

1. Place sugar cube in an old-fashioned glass and douse with 2 dashes of bitters.

2. Add water and muddle until dissolved.

3. Fill the glass with ice cubes and add whiskey.

4. Garnish with lime twist and maraschino cherry speared together on a toothpick.

Mermaid Lagoon

Complexity: 1   **Yields 1 punch bowl (serves 6)**

In clear blue pools, you can find a mermaid if you're very lucky, or perhaps very unlucky depending on the stories you believe. Anyone who comes across this refreshing, tropical lagoon of flavor will definitely want to dive right in, and risks be damned.

4 ounces blue curaçao
2 ounces melon liqueur
1 (750-milliliter) bottle prosecco
12 ounces pineapple juice
8 ounces light rum

2 (12-ounce) cans seltzer
2½ cups pineapple chunks, divided
16 stemmed maraschino cherries,
  divided
1 skewer for garnish

1. Fill a punch bowl halfway with ice.

2. Pour in blue curaçao and melon liqueur.

3. Top with prosecco, pineapple juice, rum, and seltzer.

4. Mix, and add half the pineapple chunks and 10 halved cherries.

5. Garnish punch cups with remaining pineapple and cherries, skewered.

DÜNGEONMEISTER TIP

This drink is so good that it has been known to shipwreck sailors that have heard its song coming from the jagged rocks. It has yet to be revealed how a bowl of punch could sing and who put it out on some jagged rocks in the first place. Maybe they wanted to get their drink...on the rocks.

Troll Slobber

Complexity: 1   **Yields 1 cocktail**

Out in the swamps and forests of the untamed wilderness, you can tell when you come across a troll's home from the distinctive goo left behind. Don't worry, though: This sweet and bubbly version trades in the regenerative slime for a tangy, creamy lime flavor.

2 scoops lime sherbet

2 ounces pineapple rum

5 ounces lemon-lime soda

2–3 stemmed maraschino cherries for garnish.

1. Scoop sherbet into a tall cocktail glass (such as a Collins glass).

2. Add rum and soda.

3. Stir with a cocktail spoon to create a cloudy bottom without over-stirring in order to maintain bubbles. The top should foam up. Carefully place cherries on top of the foam.

DÜNGEONMEISTER TIP

There is a rumor that the slobber of a troll can impart some of their astounding regenerative abilities to anyone brave enough to imbibe it. That rumor was started by Trandish the Bard in an attempt to trick his friend into drinking troll spit and was, by all accounts, hilarious.

Wight Russian

Complexity: 1   **Yields 1 cocktail**

Whiskey supplants vodka in this death-defying variation on the classic White
  Russian, in no small part because whiskey is the core spirit choice of intelligent undead everywhere (this isn't a joke; it's just a well-known fact—ask any
mummy). This creamy concoction will send a paralytic chill down your spine.

1 ounce chilled coffee
1 ounce coffee liqueur
1 ounce white whiskey
½ cup heavy cream
Dash orange bitters
1 orange peel

1. Combine coffee, coffee liqueur, and whiskey in an ice-filled shaker
    and shake to combine.

2. Strain into a chilled old-fashioned glass.

3. Fill with heavy cream and bitters.

4. Twist orange peel over glass to express the orange oils.

Rust Monster

Complexity: 1   **Yields 1 cocktail**

The bane of fighters everywhere, the rust monster can quickly turn even the sturdiest armor and shields to so much oxidized dust and ruin. Canny adventurers are quick to avoid these chitinous terrors, but the drink that bears their name is hard to avoid. Complexities abound in this herbal, unusual variation on the traditional rusty nail.

2 ounces mezcal
1 ounce Drambuie

Mix mezcal and Drambuie in a tumbler glass over a large ice cube.

DÜNGEONMEISTER TIP

It would be highly inadvisable to serve this particular cocktail in a mule mug, or any metal container for that matter, unless you're not thirsty and have a preponderance of paper towels around.

Chapter 6

IMMENSE INTOXICANTS

The most dangerous foes require the most delightful beverages, and that's what you'll find here. Whether you're looking for something fiery, fruity, or festive, you'll be sure to find it represented among these classically deadly foes of dungeon antiquity. You'll want to bring a whole party to face these challenges!

The 666 Layers of the Abyss, Now with Coconut

Complexity: 2   **Yields 1 cocktail**

The secret to this blended beverage lies in the dark juice of fresh cherries, which, when whirled together with coconut cream, can form beautiful striations on par with the layers of the underworld itself, each more fiendish than the one above. As an added bonus, they add a rich fruity note to the whole affair instead of the screams of an infinite army of twisted demonic wretches.

1 cup ice cubes

8–10 fresh Bing cherries, pitted

½ ounce cherry syrup

¼ cup coconut cream

2 ounces pineapple juice

2 ounces white rum

1 dollop whipped cream for garnish

1 pineapple wedge for garnish

1. Place all ingredients except whipped cream and pineapple wedge into a blender and blend on the pulse setting 15–20 seconds until combined.

2. Pour into a hurricane or other large glass.

3. Garnish with whipped cream and pineapple wedge.

DÜNGEONMEISTER TIP

This drink should never be served alongside a Nine Hells cocktail, unless you want blood all over your nice tablecloth—in which case go right ahead.

Breath Weapon

Complexity: 1   **Yields 1 cocktail**

The cunning and devious green dragons make their lairs deep in the woods, ready to spew a cloud of poison gas at any adventurers who might challenge them. While not as powerful as an ancient wyrm, this twist on the classic martini will make people take notice in a 60-foot cone.

2 ounces vodka
½ ounce dry vermouth
Splash of juice from a jar of garlic-stuffed olives
1 garlic-stuffed olive for garnish
1 clove pickled garlic for garnish

1. Combine vodka, vermouth, and garlic-stuffed olive juice in an ice-filled shaker and shake well to combine and chill.

2. Strain the mixture into a chilled martini glass.

3. Garnish with garlic-stuffed olive and pickled garlic on a toothpick.

DÜNGEONMEISTER TIP

In addition to the standard breath attack of a dragon, this drink can also imbue you with the frightful presence that wyrms are known for. Just imbibe the drink in front of someone and then start to move uncomfortably close. It's guaranteed to cause terror.

Nature Goddess

Complexity: 2   **Yields approximately 8 cocktails**

Possessed of a bountiful harvest? This cool and refreshing drink will combine the best of summer while cooling you down. Praise your nature god of choice, or at least pour a little out to keep the festering gods of decay at bay...for now.

¼ cup fresh mint leaves
1 sprig rosemary leaves
4 ounces vodka
2 cups lemon-lime soda
3 oranges, cut into wheels
1½ cups cucumber wheels

1. In a pitcher, muddle together mint and rosemary.

2. Pour in vodka and soda, and mix.

3. Create "stacks" of three or so each alternating orange and cucumber wheels, placed at the bottom of eight large cooler glasses before adding ice.

4. Pour pitcher mixture over ice into glasses and serve.

DÜNGEONMEISTER TIP

If your nature goddess is one of those "full cycle of death and rebirth" types of goddesses, this drink can be easily adapted to properly praise and raise glory unto them as well. Just alternate wheel-chopped shiitake mushrooms in among the cucumber and orange.

Claw Claw Snakebite

Complexity: 1   **Yields 1 cocktail**

One of the things besides their raw strength that makes monsters like manticores and chimeras so powerful is the fact that they have multiple means of attack. The layered attacks from this drink will definitely pack a one-two punch that is sure to be a knockout.

12 ounces dry cider
12 ounces dark beer

1. Pour cider slowly into a pint beer glass.

2. Pour dark beer over the back of a spoon slowly into glass to create a layered effect.

DÜNGEONMEISTER TIP

With the sharp claws of a lion and the powerful venom of a snake, it's no wonder people often ignore the goat part of the chimera. But that's fine. The goat part was ignoring you too. It doesn't feel bad. It likes being forgotten. Shut up. No, you're crying.

Dragon the Beach

Complexity: 1   **Yields 1 cocktail**

Dragons obviously like hitting the shore. Sure, they're mostly there to devour dolphins and unsuspecting anglers, but everyone has a different way of finding a good time. In this case, a classic beverage is brought to fiery life with a dash of spice, combining the cool of the water with the heat of the sun...and the breath weapons.

2 ounces vodka
1 ounce peach schnapps
2 ounces grapefruit juice
2 ounces cranberry juice
Dash hot honey syrup (*see recipe in Tavern Basics*)

1. Add all ingredients except hot honey syrup to an ice-filled highball glass.

2. Add hot honey syrup.

3. Stir and serve.

DÜNGEONMEISTER TIP

If you're concerned about the heat, you can always omit the hot honey syrup in favor of a dash of regular honey. At that point, however, this drink is just the classic Sex on the Beach, and I can't imagine whom that would even conceptually appeal to.

Mai Tyrant

Complexity: 2   **Yields 1 cocktail**

Distilling the essence of eyebeams isn't easy. First of all, there's, like, ten of them and they all do something different. Second, most of what they do isn't especially pleasant, drink or otherwise. No one wants a paralytic beverage or a disintegration shot, after all.

½ cup cubed seedless watermelon
3 tablespoons unspiced rum
2 tablespoons elderflower liqueur
1 tablespoon lime juice
1 tablespoon superfine sugar
4 grapes for garnish
4 bendable drinking straws

1. Put all ingredients except grapes and straws into a blender and blend on high for 30 seconds.

2. Pour into a rocks glass.

3. Garnish with grapes stuck on the end of drinking straws.

DÜNGEONMEISTER TIP

Make sure to save and reuse those drinking straws! Being bent on total mental domination of all sentient life doesn't mean you shouldn't do your part for the planet. It's the only one we've got, you know.

Purple Worm

Complexity: 2   **Yields 1 cocktail**

This beast of a beverage is as sharp-toothed and fearsome as the mind-less monster that bears its name. A deep indigo body full of berry and citrus flavors is far preferable to the half-melted slag and unfortunate miner carcasses that fill the belly of the real thing, however. Much like the colossal cnidarian, we've rimmed the mouth of the cocktail with green, but luckily it's just decorating sugar, not festering acid.

2 tablespoons green decorating sugar
2 tablespoons plus 1 ounce cranberry juice (can also use cran-grape or
 grape juice), divided
1½ ounces vodka
1 ounce blue curaçao
1 ounce sweet and sour mix
1 ounce grenadine
1 teaspoon silver luster dust

1. On a small plate, add enough green decorating sugar to cover the bottom.

2. Wet the rim of a highball glass with 2 tablespoons cranberry juice, and dip the glass into the sugar to coat the rim. Set aside.

3. Combine vodka, blue curaçao, sweet and sour mix, grenadine, remaining cranberry juice, and luster dust in an ice-filled shaker and shake vigorously to combine.

4. Fill the sugar-rimmed glass with ice and strain mixture into glass to fill.

Silver Dragon

Complexity: 2   **Yields 1 cocktail**

The silver dragon is unique among its fellows in that it is one of the few dragons that enjoys the company of human and elf, so much so that it will often transform to look like them and spend time among them. This effervescent and bubbly drink is also best in the company of friends, but, like its namesake, remains regal and often hard to find.

2 ounces dry gin
1 ounce lemon juice
1 teaspoon superfine sugar
1 large pasteurized egg white
1 (12-ounce) can club soda
1 stirring rod for garnish

1. Combine all ingredients except club soda in an ice-filled shaker and shake vigorously.

2. Strain into a chilled Collins glass and fill with club soda.

3. Serve with a stirring rod.

DÜNGEONMEISTER TIP

Oftentimes, a silver dragon will take on the shape of a human in order to participate in their favorite things, such as feasts. If you suspect there may be a dragon at your local holiday feast, try to spot the person who seems to keep putting all the silverware in a little pile in front of them.

Release the Kraken

Complexity: 2   **Yields 1 cocktail**

From the depths of the ocean comes a frightful beast that all sailors know and fear. When unleashed, there is no escaping from its grasp. Once you get a hold of this drink, you'll never want to let it out of your grasp. When the sweet and citrus flavors combine with the sour "tentacles," you'll see why the kraken is so infamous.

2 ounces dark rum
1½ ounces blue curaçao
6 ounces pineapple juice
2 ounces orange juice
1 cup ice
3–5 sour gummy worms for garnish

1. Add all ingredients except gummy worms to a blender and pulse until slushy and combined, approximately 15–20 seconds.

2. Pour drink into a cooler glass.

3. Arrange gummy worms throughout to represent tentacles.

DÜNGEONMEISTER TIP

The kraken itself has been depicted in many different forms— sometimes as a giant squid or other tentacled beast, and sometimes as a giant claymation creature from the black lagoon with four arms. Such is the mystery and majesty of the mighty beast.

Chapter 7

METAGAME MADNESS

While using metagame knowledge is usually frowned upon, these drinks based on metagame terms are sure to bring smiles. Now when the GM is responsible for a TPK, you can thank them for the tasty beverage instead of quietly cursing them and plotting how you will eventually take revenge in a satisfying way. Oh, they'll rue the day. Oh, yes. Soon. Soon.

Düngeonmeister

Complexity: 1   **Yields 1 shot**

When it comes time to proffer a drink to the one running your game, it's best to err on the side of something delicious that anyone could enjoy. This mix of liqueurs simulates a fresh cookie, in case you didn't have any homemade to give as an offering.

¾ ounce butterscotch schnapps
¾ ounce Irish cream liqueur
Splash Jägermeister
Splash cinnamon schnapps

1. Combine all ingredients in an ice-filled shaker and shake well.

2. Strain into a shot glass.

DÜNGEONMEISTER TIP

Oftentimes people will talk about pizza in relation to their GM—buying pizza, not touching the GM's pizza—all in an attempt to bribe them. I find that the better way to butter up the game master is to get them sloshed and ask for that magic item you've been wanting.

Horror Factor

Complexity: 2   **Yields 1 cocktail**

When determining just how spooky a monster is, there is a very scientific formula known as the horror factor that one can use. It takes into account all the many aspects of a thing. For example, while this drink might seem spooky at first, it is actually fairly low on the horror factor due to its blend of creamy and tangy flavors. Also, because it is a drink.

2 ounces dark rum
½ cup heavy cream
½ ounce cinnamon syrup
1 large pasteurized egg white

2 ounces sparkling apple cider
2 pinches powdered activated
  charcoal

1. Combine rum, heavy cream, syrup, and egg white in a shaker (no ice) and shake vigorously for at least 30 seconds to combine.

2. Add ice to the shaker and shake again to chill.

3. Strain into a coupe glass, and slowly fill with apple cider.

4. Top with powdered activated charcoal.

DÜNGEONMEISTER TIP

If you can't find powdered activated charcoal, do not substitute for nonactivated charcoal. We cannot stress this enough. However, the ashes of a burned ghost should suffice. Don't use any other kind of ashes, though. You'll get so haunted.

Fudge the Dice

Complexity: 2

Yields 1 cocktail

When you're on the brink of disaster and that crucial roll just won't happen, sometimes you need to fudge the roll a little. When you feel like you deserve a win, you can't go wrong with this chocolaty, decadent drink that's so good it feels like you're cheating.

1 cup crushed ice
2 scoops chocolate ice cream
1 ounce chocolate syrup
1 ounce coffee liqueur
1 ounce crème de cacao liqueur

1 ounce vodka
1 dollop whipped cream for garnish
1 stemmed maraschino cherry for garnish

1. Combine all ingredients except whipped cream and cherry in a blender and blend until smooth.

2. Pour into a stemmed glass such as a hurricane glass.

3. Top with whipped cream and cherry.

DÜNGEONMEISTER TIP

The jury is out on whether fudging the dice is an acceptable practice. Some think it's never okay. Some say it's okay only for GMs to do it in order to save the party from random chance ruining things. Still others say that if your dice are made of fudge, then they aren't going to keep very well and you should eat them immediately.

The Level Up

Complexity: 1   **Yields 1 cocktail**

Players are going to feel like celebrating when they level up; it's just the nature of the game! When it happens, why not boost those festivities with a drink that's sunny, bright, and effervescent to boot? Give them a little taste of the good life, then start throwing monsters and traps at them again.

2 tablespoons simple syrup (*see recipe in Tavern Basics*) or honey
½ cup unsweetened shredded coconut
1½ ounces pineapple juice
1½ ounces coconut juice
1 (750-milliliter) bottle champagne or sparkling wine

1. Pour enough simple syrup or honey into a small bowl to cover the bottom.

2. Dip a champagne flute in simple syrup, then roll in coconut, and set aside to set (about 1 minute).

3. Add pineapple and coconut juices to flute, then fill with champagne or sparkling wine and serve immediately.

DÜNGEONMEISTER TIP

If you're still playing an old-school game at your table, one old enough to have level drain, you'd be well advised to avoid this drink, or at least provide a bucket.

The Natural 20

Complexity: 1   **Yields 1 cocktail**

Few moments are more worthy of celebration than the one when your die clatters to a halt on that magic number, 20. It's a crit! And if a critical hit is something you're after, you'd do well to try this celebratory drink the next time you need to dig out the hit location chart to see what you've heroically separated from the bugbear. Savor the 5 percent chance of ultimate victory, which naturally is a blend of fruit and berry given complex life by the addition of a touch of the bittersweet. After all, your celebration song is some unfortunate monster's dirge.

¾ ounce citrus vodka
¾ ounce raspberry vodka
¾ ounce apple juice
¾ ounce lime juice
½ ounce simple syrup (*see recipe in Tavern Basics*)
2 dashes aromatic bitters
2 fresh blackberries for garnish

1. Combine all ingredients except blackberries in a shaker with ice and shake vigorously.

2. Strain into a chilled martini glass.

3. Spear both blackberries on a toothpick and hang them over the rim.

Never Split the Party Punch

Complexity: 1   **Yields approximately 44 ounces or 6 tall cocktails**

Veteran players know that when you are faced with a problem, you should never split the party and instead face everything as a unified team. This bubbly, sweet drink will make sure that everyone wants to gather together and no rogues go off by themselves.

12 ounces melon liqueur

8 ounces vanilla vodka

4 ounces raspberry vodka

3 ounces pineapple juice (or to taste)

3 ounces soda water or sparkling wine

12 fresh strawberry slices for garnish

1. Fill a punch bowl about halfway with ice.

2. Add all ingredients to bowl and mix well.

3. Serve in punch cups over ice.

4. Garnish each drink with 2 sliced strawberries.

DÜNGEONMEISTER TIP

The secret to a good party punch is to keep an extra amount of all the ingredients separately, not only so that you can make more punch but so that individuals can add more of anything to their own drink to make it more to their liking. Now everybody in the party is happy. Except Dan. That guy's never happy. C'mon, Dan!

Session Zero

Complexity: 1   **Yields 1 punch bowl (serves 12)**

Before really getting into the adventure, lots of groups have a Session Zero in order to establish things that they want out of the game. This refreshing and easy-to-make punch gets everybody around the table and talking to each other, the perfect start to the night.

16 ounces vodka
16 ounces silver rum
10 (12-ounce) cans beer of your choice
1 (12-ounce) can frozen lemonade concentrate
1 lemon, sliced into wheels, for garnish

1. Combine all ingredients except lemon in a punch bowl.

2. Mix with a spoon and chill until serving.

3. Garnish punch cups with 1 lemon wheel each.

DÜNGEONMEISTER TIP

Sometimes people will skip the Session Zero and get right into the thick of it. While certainly a valid way of doing things, there is something to be said for making sure that you don't show up to the group with an Orc Barbarian and your friend is a Paladin of Hating Specifically Orcs.

The TPK

Complexity: 1   **Yields 1 cocktail**

TPK stands for Total Party Kill, which is the moment at which an encounter is too overwhelming and demolishes every character without a chance.

It is brutal, it is sudden, and it will be regretted in the morning, thus the TPK. You'll need something this strong to wash defeat out of your mouth.

½ ounce vodka

½ ounce dark rum

½ ounce tequila

½ ounce gin

½ ounce blue curaçao

2 ounces sweet and sour mix

2 ounces lemon-lime soda

1 stemmed maraschino cherry for
 garnish

1. Combine all ingredients except soda and cherry in a chilled highball glass with ice.

2. Fill with soda.

3. Garnish with cherry and serve.

DÜNGEONMEISTER TIP

When facing down the sad and inevitable doom of a TPK, try to remain calm. Make yourself comfortable as the crushing enormity of your failure crashes down around you. Just remember: It's all the GM's fault. If they didn't want you to attack that dragon, they shouldn't have given it so much treasure.

Chapter 8

ALCOHOLIC ARTIFACTS

Finally, it's time for the one thing that really matters. The loot. The goods. The piles and piles of treasure that you worked so hard to get. Be careful that you make sure none of these items are too powerful, or it could unbalance your game. If you're unsure if the game is balanced, have your players walk a straight line while touching their nose and reciting the alphabet backward.

Treasure Type J

Complexity: 1   **Yields 1 cocktail**

The hard-earned reward for slaying a particularly challenging dragon, the Treasure Type J is a hoard indeed, gold shot through with yet more gold. A spicy-sweet taste of the glories that keep your party venturing into mortal danger, this cocktail is an exceptional celebration for an adventure well played.

½ ounce Goldschläger
½ ounce fresh lemon juice
3 ounces chilled sparkling wine (brut preferred)
2 dashes orange bitters

1. Pour Goldschläger and lemon juice into a champagne or martini glass.

2. Add sparkling wine and bitters.

3. Stir gently to combine.

DÜNGEONMEISTER TIP

The actual Treasure Type J is mostly the garbage left behind when a giant spider eats a bunch of farmers, and their scattered tools and copper pieces rain to the sodden cave floor below. Creative license has been applied here, as Treasure Type H, the huge mountains of gold on which dragons slumber, has a worse ring to it. No one wants to drink an H.

Astral Diamond Juice

Complexity: 2   **Yields 1 cocktail**

The astral diamond is the ultimate currency. Worth thousands of gold, unheard of by the common folk, and draped in beauty hitherto unspoken, these gems are the coin of the realm for the most powerful wizards, the most opulent demigods, and the most mythical merchants. In this recipe, we teach you how to squeeze one and drink what comes out of there.

¾ ounce Hendrick's Gin
¾ ounce crème de violette
¼ ounce blue curaçao
1 lemon wedge

3 ounces champagne or sparkling wine
1 teaspoon silver luster dust

1. Combine gin, crème de violette, and blue curaçao in a mixing glass with ice.

2. Squeeze lemon wedge into same glass and discard the peel.

3. Stir, and strain into a champagne flute.

4. Fill with champagne or sparkling wine and sprinkle the top with silver luster dust.

DÜNGEONMEISTER TIP

Though for most mortals the astral diamond is little more than a myth, that's no excuse not to flaunt one if you have it. Once you've crafted this cocktail, be conspicuous about it. And don't share it with anyone without an exchange of at least a Sun Blade or Vorpal sword.

Electrum Piece

Complexity: 2

Yields 1 shot

The rarely seen electrum piece is minted from an alloy of gold and silver, and is worth five silver pieces. Despite being half the value of a gold piece, they have a reputation in many fantasy circles akin to the two-dollar bill in that they're worth two dollars unless you're someone's weird uncle, at which point they become priceless. As a shot, they combine gold and silver in an alloy of explosive flavor that will entertain much more than any aforementioned weird uncle.

¾ ounce Goldschläger
¾ ounce energy drink
1 shake pearl luster dust
1 swizzle stick for garnish

1. Pour Goldschläger and energy drink into a shot glass.

2. Add pearl luster dust and swirl with a swizzle stick.

DÜNGEONMEISTER TIP

Dragons are known to hoard the electrum piece from time to time when forming their mighty piles to defend. This could be for a variety of reasons, from availability of gold to magical preference. Most commonly, however, it is held up as evidence that even dragons can be weird uncles.

Magic Mirror

Complexity: 2   **Yields 2 cocktails**

Magic mirrors are versatile artifacts that can let you see other places or future events, or even discern a metric of standard beauty by which one could judge someone against another. Whatever you see in this glimmering cocktail, you can be sure that the sweet flavor and unique look will make this the fairest in the land.

3 ounces white rum
3 ounces blue curaçao
½ ounce grenadine

1 teaspoon silver luster dust, divided
2 lemon twists (peels) for garnish

1. Combine rum, blue curaçao, and grenadine in an ice-filled shaker and shake to combine.

2. Strain into two cocktail glasses.

3. Add ½ teaspoon luster dust to each glass and stir to dissolve.

4. Garnish each glass with a lemon twist.

DÜNGEONMEISTER TIP

For most people, a magic mirror is one of the most important assets you could have. You can gain intel on enemy movements, spy on rival kingdoms, and see into a possible future for your endeavors. Judging a beauty contest is probably the least useful thing you could do with one.

Potion of Glibness

Complexity: 2 **Yields 1 cocktail**

Some people just don't have the gift of gab. Others merely want to improve their already decent social talents. Whatever the reason, many an adventurer has turned to a Potion of Glibness. With a sour and smooth flavor, this particular potion is sure to loosen up your lips and get the words flowing.

½ cup lemonade
2 ounces cran-raspberry juice
⅕ ounce silver rum
2 tablespoons lime juice

1. Combine all ingredients in an ice-filled shaker and shake vigorously.

2. Strain into a cocktail glass.

DÜNGEONMEISTER TIP

Nothing is worse than when you're chatting up everyone and being the life of the party and suddenly your Potion of Glibness wears off. What to do? This simple incantation can get you out of there without anyone the wiser. Verbal Component: "Wow, look at the time!" Somatic Component: Going home.

Epic Upgrade

Complexity: 3   **Yields 1 cocktail**

No one is sure when we started to accept as a society that blue is exceptional but purple is epic, but at this point in our collective experience this is an indisputable fact. If you're looking for the right libation to tout an upgrade from the above average to the extraordinary, this cocktail, which near-miraculously shifts from blue to purple before being consumed, is the way to do it. The secret lies in rapid pH alteration of the pea flower tea, so keep your flask of citric acid water handy to shift this beverage from a gin and tea to a gin and lemon in an instant.

For the Butterfly Pea Flower Tea: *6 tablespoons water*
3 grams dried butterfly pea flowers   *2 ounces gin*
1 cup hot water   *¾ ounce simple syrup (see recipe in*
For the Cocktail: *Tavern Basics)*
½ teaspoon citric acid   *1 ounce Butterfly Pea Flower Tea*

1. **For the Butterfly Pea Flower Tea:** Make the tea by adding pea flowers to hot water, steeping at least 5–7 minutes until very dark blue.

2. **For the Cocktail:** Combine citric acid and water and stir to combine, then add to a small vial or shot glass.

3. Combine gin, simple syrup, and tea in an ice-filled shaker and shake to combine.

4. Strain into a martini glass.

5. When ready to serve, add citric acid mixture to drink and watch it change color.

Pool of Radiance

Complexity: 2   **Yields 1 punch bowl (serves 8)**

Planning a spooky party or an extended dungeon run? This playful punch can add a touch of magic and mysticism to your snack table. You'll need a black light on hand, and when it's switched on you'll be presented with a glowing beverage, shot through with yet more radiant ice cubes gleaming like mystic jewels in the depths. The secret is the fluorescing quinine in tonic water, which lends the drink its distinctive bitterness. We battle that bitterness with pineapple, lime, and orange flavors, resulting in a magical phial of glowing goodness.

For the Ice:
3 cups flat tonic water

For the Cocktail:
24 ounces pisco
12 ounces Cointreau
12 ounces lime juice
12 ounces pineapple juice
7 cups tonic water

1. **For the Ice:** Fill ice cube trays with tonic water and put in the freezer 24 hours in advance.

2. **For the Cocktail:** Combine pisco, Cointreau, lime juice, and pineapple juice in a large container and stir to combine. Refrigerate until ready to serve.

3. Add juice mixture to a punch bowl and add tonic water, stirring gently to combine.

4. Add ice cubes and serve in punch glasses under your preferred black light.

Potion of Strength

Complexity: 2   **Yields 2 cocktails**

While a practiced hand and a trained body cannot be replaced with a mere potion, those wishing to give themselves the alchemical edge over their opponent will turn to potions. This bubbling dark elixir appears murky at first but hides a powerful sweetness within.

8 ounces pomegranate juice
3 ounces strawberry vodka
3 ounces black raspberry liqueur

1. Combine juice, vodka, and black raspberry liqueur in a shaker with ice and shake to combine.

2. Strain into two chilled martini glasses.

DÜNGEONMEISTER TIP

If you're going into battle and you need to be at your strongest, this is the potion for you. You may even find that the potion is too strong for you, and you will have to travel to a potion seller who sells weaker potions. If such is the case, make sure that they have respect for knights such as yourself.

US/Metric Conversion Charts

VOLUME CONVERSIONS

US VOLUME MEASURE	METRIC EQUIVALENT
⅛ teaspoon	0.5 milliliter
¼ teaspoon	1 milliliter
½ teaspoon	2 milliliters
1 teaspoon	5 milliliters
½ tablespoon	7 milliliters
1 tablespoon (3 teaspoons)	15 milliliters
2 tablespoons (1 fluid ounce)	30 milliliters
¼ cup (4 tablespoons)	60 milliliters
⅓ cup	90 milliliters
½ cup (4 fluid ounces)	125 milliliters
⅔ cup	160 milliliters
¾ cup (6 fluid ounces)	180 milliliters
1 cup (16 tablespoons)	250 milliliters
1 pint (2 cups)	500 milliliters
1 quart (4 cups)	1 liter (about)

WEIGHT CONVERSIONS

US VOLUME MEASURE	METRIC EQUIVALENT
½ ounce	15 grams
1 ounce	30 grams
2 ounces	60 grams
3 ounces	85 grams
¼ pound (4 ounces)	115 grams
½ pound (8 ounces)	225 grams
¾ pound (12 ounces)	340 grams
1 pound (16 ounces)	454 grams

OVEN TEMPERATURE CONVERSIONS

DEGREES FAHRENHEIT	DEGREES CELSIUS
200 degrees F	95 degrees C
250 degrees F	120 degrees C
275 degrees F	135 degrees C
300 degrees F	150 degrees C
325 degrees F	160 degrees C
350 degrees F	180 degrees C
375 degrees F	190 degrees C
400 degrees F	205 degrees C
425 degrees F	220 degrees C
450 degrees F	230 degrees C

BAKING PAN SIZES

AMERICAN	METRIC
8 × 1½ inch round baking pan	20 × 4 cm cake tin
9 × 1½ inch round baking pan	23 × 3.5 cm cake tin
11 × 7 × 1½ inch baking pan	28 × 18 × 4 cm baking tin
13 × 9 × 2 inch baking pan	30 × 20 × 5 cm baking tin
2 quart rectangular baking dish	30 × 20 × 3 cm baking tin
15 × 10 × 2 inch baking pan	30 × 25 × 2 cm baking tin (Swiss roll tin)
9 inch pie plate	22 × 4 or 23 × 4 cm pie plate
7 or 8 inch springform pan	18 or 20 cm springform or loose bottom cake tin
9 × 5 × 3 inch loaf pan	23 × 13 × 7 cm or 2 lb narrow loaf or pâté tin
1½ quart casserole	1.5 liter casserole
2 quart casserole	2 liter casserole

INDEX

About the Authors

Jef Aldrich is a professional podcaster from San Diego. Along with Jon, he has spent the past six years building a podcast brand outside of the big network channels. Jef started entertaining people as a SeaWorld tour guide and eventually just started being funny for a living on his own. Jef is a cocreator and cohost of the *System Mastery* podcast with Jon.

Jon Taylor is also a professional podcaster from San Diego. He has a degree in English literature from UC Santa Cruz. He spent several years as a stand-up comic on the East Coast before moving back to Southern California. Jon is a cocreator and cohost of the *System Mastery* podcast with Jef, where they review and comment on odd classic RPGs, poking fun at obscure stories and systems while taking games for a spin.